Aries

March 21 — April 19

Thru the Numbers

Aries

March 21 — April 19

by
Paul & Valeta Rice

SAMUEL WEISER, INC.

York Beach, Maine

First published in 1983 by
Samuel Weiser, Inc.
Box 612
York Beach, Maine 03910

Reprinted, 1991

Library of Congress Catalog Card Number: 82-63004

ISBN 0-87728-565-9 (Aries)

BJ

Printed in the United States of America

Depending on the year involved, the sun changes
zodiac signs on different days, consequently sources
vary in the dates they give to indicate the change-
over. Those born close to the beginning/end of a
sign are not on the "cusp" as is commonly believed.
There is a clear demarcation. If you are unsure of
your sign you may want to have your chart
calculated—or you can buy both books and see
which one works for you!

Contents

AUTHORS

If Valeta and Paul Rice sound familiar, it may be because of their extensive travel around the United States, from Alaska to the coast of California, from the East coast to Hawaii. During their invitational stopovers, they conducted workshops and seminars about Name Analysis and Birth Analysis. This continued for over twenty years until Paul's death in 1988.

Paul Rice was an engineer and Valeta a minister and psychic counselor. While their professions were very different they shared an interest in occult studies for more than 40 years, which started with their introduction to a book about ESP from Duke University. Their search for esoteric knowledge carried them into astrology, reincarnation, palmistry, tarot, color, music, I Ching, ESP, dream analysis, the qabala, yoga, structural dynamics, meditation/visualization/healing and many more sciences—techniques found both beneficial and rewarding by their clients.

They have also published *Potential: The Name Analysis Book* (Samuel Weiser, 1987) which provides an in-depth look at the special numerological nuances your name holds.

Valeta Rice still holds private consultations and is also available for lectures. She can be contacted at:

Valeta Rice
F.A.C.E. Association
177 Webster Street, #A105
Monterey, CA 93940

WHEN?

When shall I start my next project?
When should I ask for a raise?
When should I sign that contract?
When should I get married?
How will I feel when I retire?

How many times has a person looked for an answer to these questions? During this modern age the veil has been lifted on the ancient science of the vibration of the NUMBERS. This ancient science, known as the *metaphysical science of numerology,* was developed by Pythagoras, who lived in the sixth century B.C.

The simplicity of NUMEROLOGY is astounding. If you can count on your fingers you can use Numerology. It requires only a few hours study before you can begin to put to use the basic facts that you have acquired. This knowledge will give one the opportunity to see himself and other acquaintances in a better light. Apparently its simplicity is the reason Numerology was used less than other occult sciences in the past, and our society today seems to prefer complexity also.

Surprisingly, the knowledge of the numbers which govern your life will reveal many things you already know, that you had suspected or you had hoped were true.

The Numerologist takes his place alongside the Astrologer, Graphologist, Palmist and the Tarot reader, who all believe that we came into this life, not by chance, but by choice, and from these arts or sciences much can be revealed about a person's life.

Numerology reveals the vibrations in many categories including the number connected to the Birth Date, the Personal Year, the Personal Month and how the planet vibrations correlate to these numbers.

The awareness of the numbers connected to these categories helps us with a yearly and monthly course to follow.

Everyone wants to be happy and prosperous. Many unfortunate people have not learned to harmonize their birthdate vibrations with the timing of their decisions.

We are constantly called upon to make decisions which may make significant changes in our lives. Often we make the wrong decisions over family, friends, or in business because our "TIMING" is off.

The simple system of the vibration of the numbers and how they pertain to your life and the timing of your decisions will help you to come to logically deduced insights and, if carefully followed,will make you increasingly happy and prosperous throughout your lifetime.

Pythagoras, who lived twenty-five centuries ago, is considered the Father of Numbers. It is believed that he received his knowledge of the occult value of the numbers while in Egypt and Babylon. He taught these concepts and many more in his School of Occult Philosophy where the few who were allowed to attend learned how "everything can be related to numbers."

The Science of Numerology is not a quick way to happiness and achievement; it is only by becoming aware of your favorable number vibrations and then changing the unfavorable vibrations that you can smooth your pathway.

Numbers live and numbers tell and everyone can become aware of their vibrations and their relationship to themselves through the numbers.

We have explored the mundane and esoteric values of the numbers and their relationship to astrology with a lot of help from our guides.

This knowledge we wish to share with you.

ARIES

March 21st to April 19th   CARDINAL/FIRE

The RAM   Ruler: MARS

People with the BIRTH SIGN ARIES have the qualities of the RAM: leadership, fearlessness, charging ahead of the pack, leading the pack, and sometimes butting their heads against the challenges of life as they try to get through by sheer force.

All of their energies are self-directed and self-oriented. They use the "here I am" principle to assert their natural command of a situation, bringing their executive ability to bear on the solutions to life. They jump to the foreground impulsively knowing that they can take the initiative with courage to solve the immediate problem.

These self-starters of the zodiac are there at the beginning of a project, but do not expect them to be in at the ending if there is no continual challenge, as they become bored with the status quo. They need to move with speed and in doing so leave the slower acting person behind. This involves motion as well as the workings of the mind and the spirit.

Arians are the pioneers, venturing forth with strength and purpose to begin their goals.

Arousing the Aries' interest is not a difficult thing to do— KEEPING their interest alive in one direction requires expertise. Arians want freshness and aliveness in their work which they prefer to do alone or at least enough alone so that they can work out their own solutions without a hovering boss.

As they go along in their chosen profession they are interesting to watch, as they are aggressive in their dealings, competitive, wanting to be first—the winners—the tops.

When it comes to love relationships Arians embrace their lovers with enthusiasm and fiery passion which can be replaced with "Oh hum" if the relationship begins to drag or become monotonous. So spouse, lovers and roommates take heed and keep the partnership interesting and exciting if you wish to hold onto this dynamic person.

PARTNERS: A relationship with a person who has a stable BIRTH SIGN and/or BIRTH NUMBER can mediate the Aries energies so they can be focused on starting things, letting the partner assist and finish these creative drives. This fire can be used constructively when the Aries ego is held in check and a little diplomacy is used.

MARS: This planet, the ruler of Aries, is an out-thrusting energy, a positive outgoing drive that propels the Arian from the self outward. MARS is responsible for the courage to accomplish the goals Aries people set for themselves. If Arians remember the energy of their sign and the ruler of their sign they would understand themselves better. They would understand their restlessness, their impatience with slower-moving people.

CARDINAL: This is Aries' aspect of force manifesting in matter. It indicates more energy, dynamic objectives, activity, to the point, and interest in what is going on or coming down.

FIRE: The element of Aries, the virtues we bring with us to assist us in this lifetime. Here again is additional energy, ardor, emotion and the energy to originate new ideas.

NEGATIVE VIBRATIONS: Impatience, irritation with others, lack of consideration for others, a waste of energy on unimportant issues, a depletion of energy due to scattered or uncontrolled viewpoints.

NUMBERS: The NUMBER that is connected to the Aries BIRTH SIGN increases or decreases the energy of Aries. The number can increase Aries' fire and energy or add patience and stability.

HOW TO COMPUTE YOUR DESTINY

Your DESTINY, sometimes called the LIFE PATH, is the road that you as an individual travel. This is why you are here, what you should be doing in this lifetime in order to fulfill your soul. The NUMBER combined with your ARIES BIRTH SIGN reveals your soul urge, your reason for incarnating this lifetime. If you do not follow your DESTINY, you can become frustrated with unresolved goals.

Each month is represented by a number:

JANUARY	1	APRIL	4	JULY	7	OCTOBER	1
FEBRUARY	2	MAY	5	AUGUST	8	NOVEMBER	2
MARCH	3	JUNE	6	SEPTEMBER	9	DECEMBER	3

Write your BIRTHDATE on your PERSONAL CHART, page 26, using the NAME of your month—APRIL or MARCH—not the number of the month. Be sure to use the full year, i.e., 1935, NOT '35; or 1940, NOT '40, or whatever is the year of your birth. We use the "1" in the year, i.e., 1935, 1966, 1940, as well as the rest of the numbers.

On scratch paper add the number of the month, the day of the month and the year of your birth together; then reduce this number by constantly adding the numbers together until you come to a single digit or a MASTER NUMBER.

The MASTER NUMBERS are **11, 22, 33, 44, 55 and 66.**

EXAMPLE: April   9,   1935 $(1935 = 1 + 9 + 3 + 5 = 18 = 9)$
                      4   9   9 $= 22$
                      4   9   1935 $= 4 + 9 + 1 + 9 + 3 + 5 = 22$

By trying both methods you may come up with MASTER NUMBERS.

EXAMPLE: March 29, 1910 =
3   11/2 11/2 = 25/7 = **7**
EXAMPLE: March 29, 1910 = 3 + 2 + 9 + 1 + 9 + 1 + 0 = **7**
EXAMPLE: March 30, 1910 = 3 + 30 + 1 + 9 + 1 + 0 = **44**
3   3   2   = **8**

We call this last example *Research and Discovery* since we have found a *hidden* Master Number. When the Master Numbers are hidden an unexpected talent lies in the direction of the vibration of that particular number.

EXAMPLE: April 26, 1920 = 4 + 2 + 6 + 1 + 9 + 2 + 0 = **6**
EXAMPLE: 4   26   3   (1 + 9 + 2 + 0) = **33**

So, Aries, every time you find a **1, 4, 6** or **8** in your birth sign or someone else's Aries birth sign try all these methods. Then you find out if you or another person is vibrating on the Master Number or the single digit. There are persons who are content to vibrate and work on the single digit pulsation and put their talents to excellent use in that position rather than try for the esoteric vibration of the Master Numbers. This depends a lot on other numbers which concern several other categories in numerology.

The main purpose of finding your DESTINY NUMBER is to realize where you are in life's stream and learn to flow with it.

The DESTINY NUMBER and your BIRTH SIGN are two things that you cannot change. You were born on a certain day, month, and year, for you chose to be here at that time to experience what you have come to this lifetime to learn.

Another way to research and discover if you have a hidden Master Number is to add this way:

April 16, 1917 = 4 + 16 + 19 + 27 = **66**
March 18, 1926 = 3 + 18 + 19 + 26 = **66**
April 12, 1920 = 4 + 12 + 19 + 20 = **66**

The following pages will interpret the number you have chosen to go with your birth sign for this lifetime.

DESTINY NUMBER 1

Young in spirit and raring to go, Aries, number **1** gives you the creative urge to bring forth your many talents. Your original ideas must be put to work or you will be very frustrated. The RAM wants to leap ahead, as does **1**, leap-frogging over obstacles that would stop a different and more conservative sign of the zodiac.

Your quick mind moves faster with **1**, leaving your slower-paced friends behind and in chaos. Perhaps you might have to slow them down just a little if you want to keep in contact with them. If you decide to follow your creative bent then you will just move ahead at your own pace, outstripping and outdistancing others like a runner at a Marathon.

Since you are eternally optimistic, running ahead of the pack will not necessarily bother you. Develop a strength within yourself so that criticism intended to divert your attention from your goals does not get under your skin. Turn your face toward the goal and get in step with yourself.

Your personal integrity is high and since you do not want to take the time to maneuver others, your friends and associates will respect you.

1, the RAM, Aries and Mars all combine right here for leadership, aliveness, inventiveness, the very essence of life in the living and moving.

NEGATIVE: Sometimes **1** can be lonely for he prefers to handle decisions by himself without guidance from authorities. But who are the authorities anyway? Seeking assistance is fine, yet **1** is a leader so it could be better to go it alone. However, listen to others' opinions before deciding on the way to go. Emotional upheavals on the "I" of self, Aries, can bring distress if others are ignored.

Number 1

Color: Red—for energy. Project this to others.
Element: Fire—more energy. Take your vitamins.
Musical Note: C—the self-starter.

DESTINY NUMBER 2

This compassionate number can give great depths to your character, Aries. 2 is called the peacemaker and with your leadership ability and gift for thinking on your feet, you could become one of our great statesmen or stateswomen. With the entire world at unrest, diplomacy is needed in the '80s more than ever.

You have the power to concentrate on the smallest detail, although it may take a lot of your energy since you would rather be in action. When you encounter obstacles your tendency is to move away from them quickly as an Arian, yet 2 gives you the stability to stick around and try for a better agreement between arguing factions.

You can be a great trouble shooter, able to tactfully resolve both sides of a problem, partly because of the 2 and partly because your facile mind leaps ahead to solutions.

You can be an intuitive counselor for you are sensitive to others. You can bring harmony into a chaotic situation even though the RAM wants to lock horns in combat and PUSH the other person into doing it your way. Just remember that you are the diplomatic 2.

NEGATIVE: Do not expect public rewards, as your part in this schema is the KEYSTONE that others want to touch for luck. Do not depreciate your gift of reasoning instead of rushing ahead like other Arians. Your dedication to your cause will bring rich rewards of inner satisfaction for you.

Number 2

Color: Orange—for balance and harmony, the vibrant color of the sun at dawn and sunset.
Element: Water—dealing in and with the emotions; soothing the fevered brow of discontent.
Musical Note: D—for harmony and tranquility.

DESTINY NUMBER 3

This number of communication gives you the creativity of **1** plus the compassion of **2** to send forth your vibrations to others, Aries. The combination of the vibrations of **1** and **2** assists you to become more attentive to your job, your family, your distant or close friends.

This number is connected with the entertainer—one who wants to make people happy. You can express yourself in drama or comedy, projecting images to others and then acting as a catalyst, thereby assisting others to release their hopes and fears and dreams. This ability, projected through the **3** and your Mars energy, can bring others together in harmony or can send them apart. So be careful with your energy as you pick up the vibrations of those around you.

Both **2** and **3** people can be intuitive counselors but work from different levels. **2** is the compassionate patient type and **3** may use a gestalt or Socrates method of arriving at the solution for themselves or others.

As a **3** you can communicate your needs to a lover, giving of yourself joyously. Being an Aries, you are unafraid to tackle the unusual. Use your talent for words.

NEGATIVE: Guard against overacting, as the energy from your birth sign and your ruler (Mars) plus your fire element can over-whelm people and cause them to withdraw from you. Since you can pick up the rays of others and reflect a personality that is shining, watch that you do not "take over" the spotlight and invalidate another's talents.

Number **3**

Color: Yellow—for expression.
Element: Fire—more energy.
Musical Note: *E*—for feeling.

DESTINY NUMBER 4

This is the most practical number for you, Aries. **4** has a stabilizing effect in your life which will keep you from flying around this planet with no purpose. You can manifest what you want through this number, using your innate ability to begin new projects, and with the **4** you can also organize the project so it can be finished.

An Aries person is usually so full of energy that one project at a time is too boring for him; he starts many enterprises, hoping to keep interested in some of them. The **4** then gives Aries a direction toward seeing just what he is getting into.

Another wonderful aspect of the **4** is the healing potential of the hands. You can work on the etheric body if you want to take the responsibility of doing this kind of magnetic healing.

The ruler of Aries, MARS, contributes to your spontaneity. You want to get into action, don't just sit there—let's go someplace and do something! Mars in Aries, combined with **4**, gives courage and ambition without the rashness inherent in other numbers.

NEGATIVE: The impatience you have with others at times could stem from irritation with people who are not as organized as you are—and you are able to organize so fast! Many people do not have the energy you have and move a little slower both physically and mentally. You do not have to slow down for them, just realize where they are and the way they perform.

Number **4**

Color: A beautiful healing green—project this to people from your heart.
Element: Earth—another stabilizing factor, earth bound, earthy, salt of the earth, etc.
Musical Note: F—for construction, building, making things strong.

DESTINY NUMBER 5

Oh, what a good time you are going to have in 1990 or 1991, Aries, this being the travel number, the "I want to go someplace" number. It also can mean travel in your mind, study, school, and using your fire to forge ahead in many directions.

A **5** does not stand still to let life happen. He seeks life and is willing to try different approaches to make dreams come true. Albeit, he has several dreams! He is the adventurer who travels into places physically or mentally, or even into spiritual realms, delving into the unknown.

You could profit from these adventures and new experiences if you do not retreat from the new and untried—something that you do not usually do, Aries, you usually go forward with courage. This is the sensual number, relating experiences to the sensual, feeling-touching-loving-alert to fragrances and colors.

This is also the number of Creative Mind, taking the original idea and changing it into something else or something better.

Even though Arians are usually attractive to the opposite sex, the **5** Aries might double this and magnetize the opposite sex.

NEGATIVE: This seeking for variety can lead you into unhappiness if you think that you have to have a thrill every minute. However, if you can handle this, okay. Monotony can drive an Arian up the wall, or drive him to drink and hallucinogens. Self-indulgence in this way can lead to inelegance and carelessness.

Number **5**

Color: Turquoise—like a refreshing breeze. Element: Air—the breath of life. Musical Note: G—near the middle of the scale, denoting change.

DESTINY NUMBER 6

All persons who have **6** as the DESTINY number have the potential of self-realization; they have access to their higher mind through harmony. This harmonious number brings a power of logic so that a person can adjust the problems or challenges in his/her lifetime. Harmony does not just mean getting in balance yourself, it means projecting this kind, loving attention to others—listening in order to understand just what people are saying to you.

This is a great help in your profession or your chosen vocation as well as in your recreation.

This number is attuned to the metaphysical mind, Aries, and the chaos you could create by being too swift in your judgements can be tempered by just looking at what you are doing. What choices are you making? Is your energy going forth to encompass those around you or are you just forging ahead with no thought for others?

This is the cosmic mother, the one who takes care of people and things. This is the number of home, mate and family—of sharing with your loved ones.

NEGATIVE: This caring can be turned into anxiety and the desire to run everyone else's lives if your energy surges ahead too fast to control, Aries. You are quick on the draw, seeing the solution to the problem before others, literally taking their hands and showing them "how" to run their lives. Perhaps there are others who do not wish to have this close scrutiny. Don't interfere and don't become nasty when you are told, "I would rather do it myself."

Number **6**

Color: Royal blue—for stability. Meditate on this color.
Element: Earth, our planet, meaning responsibility to self and those around you. Getting "down to earth" with someone.
Musical Note: A—for receptivity. Listen for the harmony or discord in self or others.

DESTINY NUMBER 7

Most Arians live in the here and now, with a look toward the future. With this 7, Aries, you can look at the past and garner wisdom from actions taken long ago. This could take the mystical path, the thinker trying to unravel the mysteries of the universe, or this number could take you into analytical approaches toward your goals. Wisdom is the keyword. Seek hidden truths as you contemplate the metaphysical side of life and decide what path to choose to gain the most insight.

You have always wanted to be free, Aries, and 7 doubles this desire. This can take on an emotional tone where you struggle to release yourself to yourself. Yet your realistic outlook tells you that all these experiences are just learning experiences and you want to get on to the next one using your head (the Ram), to meet your obstacles and pleasures face to face.

Again, your energy drives you forward, giving you the impetus to better yourself with study, bridging from the known to the unknown and the mundane to the esoteric.

Spiritually you can take your Mars fire, red energy and use it for healing spiritual gaps in others.

NEGATIVE: Refuse to humiliate others when you are in a downward mood (which doesn't happen often). Your fine and refined approach can make you seem aloof and uncaring when all the time as a 7 you are trying to figure out what is about to happen. The aloofness could keep others away and make it difficult to communicate with you.

Number 7

Color: Violet—which stands for reverence. This lovely color can be sent for a distance for healing.
Element: Water—looking at your reflection while crossing the bridge from the known to the unknown and understanding this trip.
Musical Note: B—for reflection.

DESTINY NUMBER 8

This is the number for power, Aries. This is where you find yourself in a leadership position, directing other people, handling money and directing the disposition of it, if you are working on the positive side of the number and using your Mars-directed energy realistically. If you are flying away in never-never land, full of idealistic fantasies and not putting your good mind and steward-ship to practical use, then you are not aware of your full capabilities. Power can be used for good, to bring others to the realization that they CAN handle themselves, their jobs, their families and their mates with justice and love—sharing instead of trying to make everything come out 50-50.

On the esoteric level, you have the opportunity in this lifetime to open or re-open your third eye. This means many things, in-cluding an awareness of other people's energy and how it affects you, so you can handle the flow. You could learn to see auras and assist others to discover where their energies lie.

The main energy of **8** combined with Aries is a practical application of your knowledge. The Mars fire can assist you to know that you can take charge of large corporations, etc.

NEGATIVE: Here is the schemer; the one who loves glory and fame and attention without really deserving it. If you have put in lots of study, etc., then achieve your rewards—good, this becomes a fact. If you have plotted and walked over others to gain money, position, glory, and fame, then you really are not entitled to the adulation. Watch your intolerance, Aries. Do not become impa-tient when you are not able to get your own way. As an **8** you can get there because you are the natural leader.

Number **8**

Color: Rose—the color of love.
Element: Earth—for achievement on this third dimension, this earth, material gain.
Musical Note: High C—for research.

DESTINY NUMBER 9

Aries, this is the number that represents the servers of mankind. Your Mars fire reaches out for the universal truths so that you can free yourself from personal restrictions. You can go beyond the self-seeking to expand your horizons, able in time to transcend your bias toward other ideas, other races or other belief systems.

This is brotherly love, recognizing that all persons are in need of strokes of love, all persons have unique experiences which compel them to act as they do. This all-encompassing love can spread out to all those you meet and inspire them to act with love and compassion for their fellow man (or woman).

Your emotional attachments to individuals may be short but intense as you move from one person to another. These intense relationships may bring frustration to others but in time they will realize that you do not want to possess them. You inspire others and then set them free.

Your destiny is to be working in the mainstream of life where you can be an instrument for good, bringing love and desire for a better world to many people.

Awareness and success are keywords to remember. This is the number of completion, getting the job done, finishing tasks, staying with the project.

NEGATIVE: You could rush forward, Aries, carrying the flag of redemption in your zeal and find no one behind you to carry on your work unless you face facts and operate with practicality. If your zeal is thwarted too often you may become bitter and blame others for not seeing your goals. Discretion is the keyword.

Number 9

Color: Yellow-gold—for perfection, or the desire to make everything perfect (in your opinion). At least take time to look at the other fellow's opinion before you go striding off into the sunset, followed by no one. You can change things with realistic love.

Element: Fire—for warmth. People like to be around you, Aries, for you inspire others to be more than they think they are.

Musical Note: High D—for accomplishment.

DESTINY NUMBER 11

This is the first MASTER NUMBER after all the single digits from 1 through 9. All Master Numbers carry a responsibility for they are higher vibrations of the single digit they reduce to. For example: $11 = 1 + 1 = 2$. So **11** should be correctly written **11/2** to show that a person could be vibrating on either or both levels. This holds true for all the other master numbers.

This number is for the perfectionist; intuition can develop the mind to a genius level. The search for truth can raise the level of personal intelligence as well as that of others if a desire to share what is learned is present.

Sometimes **11** is reluctant to do this, feeling that if he knows "about something" then everyone else "knows about" it too. Aries, take note that you may discover new and exciting ways to examine your way of life, your job, your family or your mate. Share this knowledge and intuition with whom it may concern if you want to bring a better understanding between you and those who are important to you.

You will receive dreams and flashes of illumination which could light the path for many to follow. Your perceptions can influence those around you and even change the consciousness of humanity for the better.

NEGATIVE: Since you are intuitively brilliant and your goals are inspiring, your fame can overwhelm you if you turn to greed. This is the trap for many a genius who became self-superior and fanatical about his mission in life. Some keep their discoveries to themselves, enriching no one.

Number **11**

Color: Silver—for attraction. You can magnetize other people to your support.
Element: Air—for the idealist who builds fantasies and pictures in the air. Don't knock it, fantasies can become realities.
Musical Note: High *E*—for magnetism.

DESTINY NUMBER 22

This Master Number brings your high flying energy down to practical application as it is the number of physical mastery over your own body. You have the ability to use the higher vibrations to heal bodies by laying on hands. Search this metaphysical vibration very thoroughly, Aries, to discover where the healing comes from and how to handle it. There are many theories to evaluate before you decide which one is the most comfortable for you.

Spiritually you need to harness your Mars fire to learn service on a constructive basis, a much larger scale than the reduction to **4** (the work number).

You can use an international direction, entering into politics, managing large corporations, becoming the nation's foremost diplomat, or in many other directions which coincide with your Mars fire and your Aries energy to sustain your physical stability. You need to have and keep a healthy body to sustain the pressures that seem to be part of the job of positions in high authority.

Your self-mastery can be expanded to opportunities to show others how discipline can be used to improve conditions on our planet.

Think of **22** as being a double **11**, the idealism of **11** projected into international realms. If you are not ready for this heady vibration, then operating on a **4** level could bring the manifestation of your desires to fruition. If you think you can do it, you can, with a little effort thrown in.

NEGATIVE: You could feel unfulfilled, Aries, if you do not attempt to reach farther than your work-a-day world. If you do not follow through with your grandiose plans you will become known as the big talker, not the doer.

Number **22**

Color: Red-gold—for practical wisdom. Use the things you have learned for practical application, not dreams.
Element: Water—for cleansing. Clean out the fantasies from your life and see reality.
Musical Note: High F—for physical mastery over self.

DESTINY NUMBER 33

This Master Number may be a difficult one for you to handle, Aries, until you learn how to handle your emotions. When you learn how the emotions work to control your life then you truly can be the emotional master, able to quell groups of people who are fomenting trouble, providing you have the knowledge of how to handle emotional groups. This requires study and lots of patience to understand the power that you can wield.

Your Mars fire wants to rant and rave over injustices to yourself personally or to others, yet you have the rare opportunity to learn how to count to three before acting (count to six if the situation is almost out of control).

Think of **33** as being the combination of **11** and **22**. **11** is the idealist who wants perfection in all things and **22** is the practical master who can really put this idealism to use. The combination leads to **33** which would be using feeling to get the job done!

22 knows that the plan can get to be perfect if effort is applied in the right direction (perfection—**11**). Realizing this, a **33** can bring a balance to disagreements by using humor in small doses.

Fortunately, our present metaphysical knowledge contains information about the emotions and what to do about minus emotions such as "hate," "anger," etc.

Use your Mars fire of love as you surge forward (*the Ram*) in your endeavors.

NEGATIVE: You could fall into the trap of trying to control others since you have leadership qualities. Or you could become emotionally impoverished and apathetic towards others. Be particular in your choices of goals for you can sway people through their emotions.

Number **33**

Color: Deep sky-blue—for intensity. Your feelings are on the surface, your face and actions show this.
Element: Water—for emotional mastery, flowing with or controlling the stream.
Musical Note: High G—for emotional healing.

DESTINY NUMBER 44

If you thought **8** was powerful just look at this number and what it brings, Aries. This is double power and is the Master Number of the mental body. The MIND is a complex structure containing receptors (the way we see and perceive things), reactors (the way we react to different stimuli), and analytical functions. The mental body uses the latter part of the mind (the analytical portion).

You can approach a challenge through the analytical doorway, look at the facts, then use your inherent abilities to forge ahead in your thinking to discover certainties and uncertainties. With these facts, you can then arrive at a conclusion.

33, on the other hand, approaches challenges through FEELING and reacting emotionally. Think of **44** as being a double **22** with more under your leadership and fire of ambition. Also think of **44** as being a combination of **11** and **33** and you get a little different twist. **11** is the idealist and **33** is the emotional master or the ability to become the master of the emotions.

NEGATIVE: This amount of power would be difficult for some birth signs to handle. Already being the leader, Aries, and with the fire of Mars, you can handle this much power if you do not become too rigid in your opinions with the attitude "I am always right because I am always right." Maybe you are, but does this get the job done, or does it cause problems to others and send them into confusion? The lowest vibration of this Master Number is to try to control other people through mental cruelty. Here is the psychotic who controls people by using his mask of righteousness in front of and behind the scenes. Be careful of your camouflage, Aries.

Number 44

Color: Blue-green—for tranquility. This color calms the intense fire of ambition and helps put it in the right perspective.
Element: Earth—for mental mastery.
Musical Note: High A—for mental healing.

DESTINY NUMBER 55

Since most Arians are full of life, it may seem strange that you chose to come into this lifetime with the number of LIFE ENERGY. This number brings you the task of bringing light and life to others by looking toward the future so you can excite others about coming events and projects.

At this level you can be a channel, bringing light and knowledge from higher dimensions into the consciousness of those ready to receive this inspiration.

As light from the sun beams down to the earth, breaking through the prism of consciousness to become warmth, intelligence and tranquility, so does a **55** (if willing) act as a prism to bring understanding to us from higher dimensions.

Think of **55** as being a combination of **22** and **33** added together, wherein the practical mastery of things on this plane of existence works with the mastery of emotions to bring a moving life energy force into existence to elevate the consciousness of all those with whom you contact with this energy.

Or think of **55** as being a combination of **11** and **44**, wherein the dreamer (**11**) designs a world of his/her own and is able to make it take form (come true) through the double powerful energy and command of **44**.

NEGATIVE: If you choose this side of the number, Aries, you are karma-burdened with inaction on the right path. Choose to look forward in a positive manner instead of wallowing in self-pity. This is where the victims of life are still walking in darkness, seeing no light or path.

Number 55

Color: Red-violet—the abundant life energy.
Element: Air—for spirituality. Discover the way of the masters. Meditate.
Musical Note: Chord of G—for spiritual healing.

DESTINY NUMBER 66

This is a powerful number, Aries, and can be found by the Research and Discovery method, page 10. This number radiates love energy; it is a Master Number which carries a great deal of power in Love.

This love extends from self to others, Aries, knowing that one cannot love others unless you know and recognize the perfection of one's own soul. This is not an ego trip; it is a full realization of outpouring love through the acceptance of karma-free relationship in soul. The inner self receives a vision of perfection and yearns for this love relationship with the soul mate and the supreme being.

You can seesaw between the Master Number **66** and **3**, which is its reduction, sometimes feeling this love and sometimes just wanting to entertain people with humor and aliveness, Aries.

66 is truly the cosmic mother, the double six leading to the nine: i.e., $6 \times 6 = 36$, or $3 + 6 = 9$, brotherly love.

You are here to keep the love flame going and we don't mean sex, although that is a part of it. We are speaking of the joy in the total universe.

NEGATIVE: If your temper gets in the way, Aries, you can use this love as a tool to enslave another. Jealousy can rear its ugly head and you can become determined to get even. If this number is used on the negative side you can refuse love through anger, or even become selfish and possessive of your mate, your friends, or your things.

Number **66**

Color: Ultra-rose—meditation on this color will open the heart chakra more fully.

Element: Fire—for burning away the dross, the contempt, the frustration, the hate, and bringing forth the imprisoned love for self and others.

Musical Note: Any chord struck in harmony that can bring you in balance. Find the particular chord to which you vibrate.

YOUR PERSONAL CHART

Birthdate _____
Birth Number_____
Birth Sign_____
Birth Element_____

This planetary aspect represents the moral excellence and goodness that the soul has achieved in former lifetimes, virtues which will assist a person in this lifetime.

Birth Musical Note_____

Personal Year for 1991_____
Personal Year for 1992_____
Personal Year for 1993_____
Personal Year for 1994_____
Personal Year for 1995_____
Personal Year for 1996_____
Personal Year for 1997_____
Personal Year for 1998_____

Personal Month Numbers:

January _____
February _____
March _____
April _____
May _____
June _____

July _____
August _____
September_____
October _____
November _____
December _____

Challenges:

Major_____
1st Sub-challenge_____
2nd Sub-challenge_____

PERSONAL YEAR

The PERSONAL YEAR NUMBER is the vibration that influences your life in any given year. This is a fine focus of JUPITER, the planet of benevolence and idealism. Jupiter showers you with all the good things of life as long as you recognize what the good things are. If you are operating on the negative side of Jupiter, it could lead you into extravagance and greediness.

To obtain this number you add your BIRTH MONTH and your BIRTH DAY to the year you are seeking. For example: If your birth date is March 16, 1955, and you want to find the PERSONAL YEAR for 1980 you do this:

Add 3 (March) to 16 (the day) to 1980 = 1999;
1999 = 1 + 9 + 9 + 9 = 28; 28 = 2 + 8 = 10
10 = 1 + 0 = **1** PERSONAL YEAR for the year 1980 for the birth date of March 16, 1955.

Do not use your own birth year; use the year in which you wish to find your PERSONAL YEAR.

PERSONAL MONTH

Still under the influence of that great planet, JUPITER, we also find our own PERSONAL MONTH by adding our PERSONAL YEAR to the current month or the month we are seeking.

Example: March 16, 1955 is the birth date. We want to find the PERSONAL MONTH for July 1980. Since we have already established the PERSONAL YEAR for this birth date for 1980 as **1,** we simply take the **1** and add it to the month of July, which is represented by **7**.

1 (Personal Year) + **7** = **8** (Personal Month).

TABLE OF PERSONAL MONTHS

JUPITER: EXPANSION, UNDERSTANDING, FRIENDLINESS, ABUNDANCE, INSPIRATION, INCREASE, SPUR.

The definitive words for Jupiter listed above captured the essence of the positive side of Jupiter's vibrations. Understand these words by using a good dictionary as you discover the true meaning for yourself. Meditating on all the descriptive words given in this booklet will assist you also.

The NEGATIVE side of the JUPITER vibration is: EXTRAVAGANCE, INDULGENCE, CYNICISM, GREED.

When we talk about the TIMING of your decisions we need to remember that Jupiter has an influence as well as the vibration of the number that you find for your own PERSONAL MONTH. The interpretations for personal months are as follows:

PERSONAL MONTH 1

This is a time for action, a time to seek new, exciting offers which could enhance your position in your profession, relationships with your mate or with your family or in your search for the wellness aspect for your physical body, your mind or your spirit, Aries. Be sure to check how this agrees with your Personal Year by reading the interpretations of the NUMBERS on pages 36 thru 39. By putting the two readings together you will become aware of what is happening in your life and how to determine the forward positive movement you can take at this time. Use your Mars fire to further your ambitions and welcome opportunities that come your way this month, Aries. This could mean a change of job, a new lover, a new physical home or a change of attitude toward your life. Act on your intuition and take charge of the direction in which you are moving. This is an opportune time to make full use of the Mars fire of ambition to find the unusual.

NEGATIVE: You could become bossy and arrogant over your successes this month, thereby incurring the wrath of your associates. Watch it.

PERSONAL MONTH 2

Good relationships can be formed during this month, Aries, if your Destiny Number is compatible. Always look at your Destiny Number to see how it goes with your Personal Year and Month vibration so that you are in harmony. Friendships will come to you but it is up to your Aries nature to find the spark to ignite the fire which can cement the real feeling between you and the person or circumstance. You can let a month like this give you a quiet time, a resting period to build up your intense energy, Aries. Small issues may assume inflated importance during a 2 month, so delay your decisions until next month if it is at all possible. Jupiter's kindness, consideration for others, and optimism is prevalent at this time, so seek understanding of the values of life.

NEGATIVE: Using this month to be more by yourself to examine your pathway is not a selfish vibration. If your quiet time includes criticism of others and sends you on a downtone, indulging in fantasies to detract from another's personality—that is negative.

PERSONAL MONTH 3

Good relationships can be formed in this month also, but the perspective is different—that of communicating to others in your inspiring way, Aries. Accept invitations or have friends over for a good time, an evening of play or exhilarating games. Display your talents if you are seeking new friends, Aries. Go forward, do not look into the past; you have already lived those lifetimes and it is a time to look into the future, make your plans and secure your goals. It is easy for you to be light-hearted, Aries, use this talent to lift others up to this fun level. Laughter cures a lot of ills and we all tend to be more serious than we need be. Communication is very important at this time, listen and talk until you understand just what is going on in your job. This job may concern family or business.

NEGATIVE: Exaggerations and alibis lead nowhere during this month. Face the facts. If you have become conceited about your accomplishments, Aries, try not to communicate this to others.

PERSONAL MONTH 4

Well, down to earth again and to work, Aries. This month is an opportunity to put your house in order. This means your physical surroundings, ending the cycles that you started in a 1 year or month if this is at all possible. 4 months also give you a chance to take inventory of your belongings, your attitudes, your relationships and your progress on the path you have chosen for this lifetime. Where are you going? Are you satisfied with the life you are leading? With the friends with whom you have surrounded yourself by choice? When you have completed the inner workings, plan ahead. Organize and analyze the details of contracts, correct errors, put your correspondence and your finances in order. Stabilize yourself this month as next month brings some exciting adventures which fit your vibrant self, Aries. Cut and prune away the deadwood to discover the true flower of sanity.

NEGATIVE: If you have become rigid in your opinions and unwilling to give up "your way," now is the time to find out why you are inflexible on certain matters.

PERSONAL MONTH 5

Jupiter's influence is really with you this month, for EXPANSION is in the air. Adventure, travel and moving in several directions at once, Aries. This is compatible with your energies and should be a fun time for you as you move rapidly into unusual situations. This is a time of activity, creating new images through your Mars fire. In business this is the month to advertise, to contact many people and also open your mind to many different ideas. This is a stretching time, looking at many different viewpoints—not necessarily making decisions—just experiencing change and more change. Discard your old ideas if they have not been productive.

NEGATIVE: This can be a restless month where you hop from one circumstance to another, creating havoc instead of acquiring more wisdom. Keep yourself well-groomed, as the tendency to become so involved with whatever can make you careless and sloppy.

PERSONAL MONTH 6

Home is where we live and it is very important to recognize your roots this month, Aries. Attend and serve those closest to you even though it takes patience to listen to their tales of woe. Give your family, whether it be your mate, lover, children or a group, your loving attention and friendliness. This is a personal time for you to listen to the inner guidance and use this perception to clue into other people's feelings so you can be of some help. This help means not taking on their burdens but assisting them with love to see what their real problem is, and turn it into an asset. Establish harmony with those around you and protect those who need your energy. Being as self-realized as you are, Aries, you can turn to the doorway of higher mind through harmony. Bring yourself in balance and turn on your love when meditating so you can contact your higher self.

NEGATIVE: This is the month for anxieties and carelessness if you practice pridefulness and cynicism on your family.

PERSONAL MONTH 7

This month balance your checkbook and all your accounts. The analytical approach will carry you far this month, Aries. Insist on freedom from worry all this month. Try to be alone part of the time so you can get your thoughts and desires in balance. Keep yourself in control, don't be sloppy in your appearance, your walk, your words or your surroundings. Dust off those knick-knacks you haven't found time to look at lately, and while you are at it, dust off some of your outmoded ideas.

NEGATIVE: You may become skeptical and aloof from your friends because of this need to be alone. Don't let confusion over the issues suppress your naturally exuberant self.

PERSONAL MONTH 8

This is a power month for you, Aries, a time to take a good look at your money situation. Have you done your homework about how you can make money so that this month you can collect on your knowledge, your expertise? Is your energy directed toward gathering in your rewards? 8 also symbolizes glory which could be the opening or re-opening of your third eye. The third eye is the director of energy; it is the inner vision. Practice the power of visualization during this time to assist the opening. This month will also bring rewards both emotional and material. Think big, organize yourself toward the goals you wish to accomplish. Aim your sights high and receive.

NEGATIVE: Money and power could slip through your fingers if you scatter your energy this month. Try not to become impatient or unjust.

PERSONAL MONTH 9

A wonderful month to clean up your debts, clean your closets, finish your projects so that next month you can begin anew. Complete as many cycles as you can or have time for. This is the month to use that wonderful energetic Mars energy to get things done, Aries. Be charitable toward others as you bustle about. This is a good time for public appearances and performances, especially those which are involved with community affairs and any meetings that concern human affairs. It is time to express your love for your mate in realistic ways, gifts, unusual treats, love and sharing.

NEGATIVE: You could find yourself just doing for yourself instead of sharing your love. Sometimes impersonal love—just for mankind—and service brings good feelings, Aries. Don't neglect your friendships at this time. Center on others instead of self.

CHALLENGES OF LIFE

CHALLENGES are obstacles we encounter during this lifetime. We are now concerned with the timing of events that stop you from progressing until you understand just what the obstacle is and means.

In the FIRST HALF of your lifetime, you will encounter a SUB or minor challenge which is represented by a number.

In the SECOND HALF of your lifetime, you will encounter a SUB or minor challenge which is represented by a number.

The MAJOR CHALLENGE, also represented by a number, is with you your entire lifetime until you solve the mystery. We accepted these challenges when we decided to incarnate on this planet so that we can strengthen the weak links in our destiny. Recognizing these weak links by finding the negative influences of these numbers will be helpful.

SATURN is the planet known as the DISCIPLINARIAN, the teacher, the door to the initiation and all these good things we shy away from or fear. See Saturn's other side—if you have no game going, no challenge and life proceeds smoothly straight down the road with the same scenery—where is the spice? Understand the good that Saturn brings us. Saturn is connected to the challenges of life.

FIRST SUB CHALLENGE: Subtract the number of your birth MONTH from the number of your birth DAY or vice versa.

SECOND SUB CHALLENGE: Subtract the number of your birth DAY from your reduced birth YEAR or vice versa.

MAJOR CHALLENGE: Subtract the FIRST SUB CHALLENGE from the SECOND SUB CHALLENGE or vice versa. Place all these numbers in your PERSONAL CHART on page 26.

EXAMPLE: April   6, 1944
            4   6   9
           _____
                 2   3   = **2** is the First Sub Challenge
                      1   **3** is the Second Sub Challenge
                              1 is the Major Challenge

TABLE OF CHALLENGES

1—Many people will try to dominate and control your life. The remedy is choosing your own way without being belligerent about it. Know when you are right and please yourself after considering all the facts. Strengthen your self-determinism and be the daring, creative person you really are. Dependence on others can limit your talents.

2—Your feelings are uppermost and you are apt to turn others' opinions into personal affronts. This sensitivity can be very useful if you "tune" into people and see where they are. Cultivate a broader outlook on life and learn to be cooperative without being indecisive. Be thoughtful and consider the welfare of others as well as your own.

3—Social interaction frightens you and your reaction is to withdraw or become the loud overreactor. Each violent swing of the pendulum suggests that you are living in a personal construct without reality. Develop your sense of humor; try painting, dancing, writing or any artistic sort of self-expression that can bring out the real you.

4—This easy challenge is LAZINESS! However it can lead you into a rut where it is too much trouble to get out of that comfortable chair to answer the phone. Finish your cycles of activity and you will find your energy level rising. The other side of this challenge is rigidity. Learn patience and tolerance without becoming a slave.

5—This "freedom" number allows us to progress BUT it does not mean doing anything and everything we desire without paying attention to our responsibilities. There are laws of society and universe that tell us to use moderation, not overindulgence, in sex, drugs, alcohol or food. Organize your life. Recognize duties to family and friends.

6—This idealistic number may lead you into thinking that you have the best of all possible answers and belief systems. Your opinions can be dogmatic where personal relationships are at the crossroads. Do not impose your "perfection" on others. Give willingly of your time and knowledge without suppressing others' creativity. Turn "smug" into "hug."

7—This research and discovery number challenges you to become scientific and analytical. Heed your inner guidance. Develop a patience with existing conditions and make an effort to improve them. Do not stifle your spiritual nature. Your limitations are self-imposed. Cultivate faith in the justice of the general plan of things then seek to better it.

8—Wastefulness is the keyword for **8**. This can be brought about by carelessness or miserliness. A false sense of values, efficiency and judgements can become fetishes in the material world. Use your energies to cultivate good human relationships and avoid greed. Be guided by reason and not by avarice. Honor, glory, fame and money are okay if acquired in the right way.

9—This challenge is rare since it carries the lack of emotion and human compassion. It also means judging others and refusing to understand them because of an inflated ego. The time has come for this person to learn to love and empathize with others.

0—Here is NO or ALL challenges. Study all the NUMBERS above and see if you react to one. You have reached a point in your spiritual development where you can choose which challenge to release. Smooth the edges, learn and know the vibrations of the independence of **1**; the diplomat of **2**; the emotional thrust of **3**; the diligence of **4**; the expansion of **5**; the adjustment of **6**; the wisdom of **7**; the power of **8**; and the Universal Brotherhood of **9**.

If your CHALLENGES are the same as your DESTINY NUMBER, give it very close scrutiny.

NUMBERS

Every number can be expressed on three levels—
POSITIVE—NEGATIVE—REPRESSIVE. This does not mean that a
person is expressing on all three levels. You can evaluate yourself
by observing:

1. How you react in certain situations.
2. What is your chronic emotional tone?
    Happy, grumpy, short-tempered, enthusiastic,
    fearful, bored, etc.?
3. Check how the interpretations listed below
    represent your over-all response to your daily grind.

POSITIVE	NEGATIVE	REPRESSIVE
Certain	Apathetic	Despotic
Enthusiastic	Unsure	Tyrannical
Definite	Antagonistic	Suppressive
Specific	Vacillating	Hostile
Searching	Non-feeling	Violent
Transforming	Covert	Stop Motions
Activating	Resentful	Hateful

This is the reason that people with the same numbers react
differently to certain situations and differ in attitude towards
themselves and others. You can choose which level you are now
on and change your level if you wish to change yourself. You can
also change your name or a few letters of your name to bring in
the vibrations of your choice.

See our book on Name Analysis—POTENTIAL! This book
gives you an in-depth analysis of your personality. It is soon to be
available at book stores or can be ordered direct from the Rices.

Number **1**:
POSITIVE: Creative; optimistic; self-determined; creative mind
through feeling; can reach a higher dimension of awareness when
preceded by a **10**.
NEGATIVE: Indecisive; arrogant; fabricator.
REPRESSIVE: Tyrannical; hostile; ill-willed.

Number **2**:
POSITIVE: Sensitive; rhythmic; patient; a lover; restful; a peacemaker; skilled; responsive to emotional appeal with love; protective.
NEGATIVE: Impatient; cowardly; overly sensitive.
REPRESSIVE: Mischievous; self-deluded; hostile.

Number **3**:
POSITIVE: Communicative; entertaining; charming; can acquire knowledge from higher beings; inspirational; an intuitive counselor.
NEGATIVE: Conceited; exaggerating; dabbling but never really learning anything exactly; gossiping.
REPRESSIVE: Hypocritical; intolerant; jealous.

Number **4**:
POSITIVE: Organizer; devoted to duty; orderly; loyal; able to heal etheric body by magnetism; works on higher levels; endures.
NEGATIVE: Inflexible; plodder; penurious; stiff; clumsy; rigid; argumentative.
REPRESSIVE: Hateful; suppressive; gets even.

Number **5**:
POSITIVE: Adventurous; understanding; clever; knows the essence of life; creative mind on the mental level; traveler; creative healer.
NEGATIVE: Inconsistency; self-indulgence; sloppy; tasteless; inelegant.
REPRESSIVE: Perverted; afraid of change; indulgence in drink, food, dope; no sympathy.

Number **6**:
POSITIVE: Harmonious; good judgement; love of home and family; balance; cosmic mother; self-realization; the doorway to higher mind through harmony.
NEGATIVE: Anxious; interfering; careless.
REPRESSIVE: Cynical; nasty; domestic tyranny.

Number **7**:
POSITIVE: Analytical; refined; studious; capable of inner wisdom; symbolizes the bridge from the mundane to the esoteric; the mystic; able to heal spiritual gaps.

NEGATIVE: Confused; skeptical; humiliates others; aloof; a contender.
REPRESSIVE: Malicious; a cheat; suppressive to self and others.

Number 8:
POSITIVE: Powerful; a leader; director; chief; dependable; primal energy; can open third eye; money maker; sees auras.
NEGATIVE: Intolerant; biased; scheming; love of power—fame—glory without humility; impatient.
REPRESSIVE: Bigoted; abusive; oppressive; unjust.

Number 9:
POSITIVE: Compassionate; charitable; romantic; aware; involved with the brotherhood of man; successful; finisher; merciful; humane.
NEGATIVE: Selfish; unkind; scornful; stingy; unforgiving; indiscreet; inconsiderate.
REPRESSIVE: Bitter; morose; dissipated; immoral.

Number 11:   IDEALIST
POSITIVE: Idealistic; intuitive; cerebral; second sight; clair-voyant; perfection; spiritual; extrasensory perception; ex-cellence; inner wisdom.
NEGATIVE: Fanatic; self-superiority; cynic; aimless; pragmatic; zealot.
REPRESSIVE: Dishonest; miserly; carnal; insolent.

Number 22:   PHYSICAL MASTERY
POSITIVE: Universal power on the physical level; financier; cultured person; international direction in government; physical mastery over self.
NEGATIVE: Inferiority complex; indifference; big talker—not doer; inflated ego.
REPRESSIVE: Evil; viciousness; crime on a large scale; black magic.

Number 33:   EMOTIONAL MASTERY
POSITIVE: The idealist with power to command or serve; leader who has emotions under control; constructive emotionally con-trolled ideas.
NEGATIVE: Erratic; useless; unemotional; not using his/her gifts of sensitivity to others.

REPRESSIVE: Power to work on other people's emotion to their detriment; riot leaders.

Number **44**:   MENTAL MASTERY
POSITIVE: Universal builder with insight; can institute and assist world-wide reform for the good of mankind; can manifest his postulates.
NEGATIVE: Mental abilities used for confusion of worthwhile ideas; twists meanings of great statesmen and very able people for personal use.
REPRESSIVE: Crime through mental cruelty; uses mask of righteousness to do evil; psychotic.

Number **55**:   LIFE ENERGY
POSITIVE: Abundant life; channels from higher dimensions with ease; brings light into existence; student of action; heals using life force.
NEGATIVE: Karma burdened with inaction on the right path; chooses to look backward and wallow in self-pity.
REPRESSIVE: Victim of life; in darkness; no path visible; withdraws; blames others.

Number **66**:   LOVE ENERGY
POSITIVE: Self-realization through love; this love extends from self to others, knowing that one cannot love others unless one knows and recognizes the perfection of one's own soul.
NEGATIVE: Using love as a tool to enslave another; extreme selfishness and possessiveness; refusing love when time and person is correct.
REPRESSIVE: Seeing only the barriers to love; repressing loving attention to others; repressing the need to outpour cosmic love to others.

BIBLIOGRAPHY

Avery, K., *Numbers of Life*, Freeway Press
Bailey, A., *Esoteric Healing*, Lucis Pub. Co.
_____,*From Intellect to Intuition*, Lucis Pub. Co.
_____,*Initiation: Human and Solar*, Lucis Pub. Co.
_____,*Letters on Occult Meditation*, Lucis Pub. Co.
_____,*Problems of Humanity*, Lucis Pub. Co.
_____,*Telepathy*, Lucis Pub. Co.
Campbell, F., *Your Days are Numbered*, Gateway
Diegel, P., *Reincarnation and You*, Prism Pubs.
Fitzgerald, A., *Numbers for Lovers*, Manor Books
Johnson, V., & Wommack, T., *Secrets of Numbers*, Samuel
        Weiser, Inc.
Jordan, J., *Romance in Your Life*, DeVorss & Co.
_____,*Your Right Action Number*, DeVorss & Co.
Leek, S., *Magic of Numbers*, Collier-MacMillen, Pubs.
Long, M.F., *Growing into Light*, DeVorss & Co.
_____,*Huna Code in Religions*, DeVorss & Co.
_____,*Secret Science Behind Miracles*, DeVorss & Co.
_____,*Secret Science at Work*, DeVorss & Co.
_____,*Self Suggestion*, DeVorss & Co.
Lopez, V., *Numerology*, New American Library, Inc.
Rice, P. & V., *Potential! Name Analysis,* Samuel Weiser, Inc.
_____,*Timing*, F.A.C.E.
_____,*Triadic Communication*, F.A.C.E.
_____,*Thru the Numbers*, Samuel Weiser, Inc. (a series for each
        zodiac sign)
Roquemore, K.K. *It's All in Your Numbers*, Harper & Row
Schure, E., *Pythagoras and the Delphic Mysteries*,
        Health Research
Street, H., Taylor, A., *Numerology, its Facts and Secrets*,
        Wilshire Book Co.
Thommen, G. S., *Is this your Day?*, Crown Publishing Co.

YOUR PERSONAL CHART

Birthdate _____

Birth Number _____

Birth Sign _____

Birth Element _____

This planetary aspect represents the moral excellence and good-
ness that the soul has achieved in former lifetimes, virtues which
will assist a person in this lifetime.

Birth Musical Note _____

Personal Year for 1991 _____

Personal Year for 1992 _____

Personal Year for 1993 _____

Personal Year for 1994 _____

Personal Year for 1995 _____

Personal Year for 1996 _____

Personal Year for 1997 _____

Personal Year for 1998 _____

Personal Year for 1999 _____

Personal Year for 2000 _____

Personal Month Numbers:

January _____   July _____

February _____   August_____

March   _____   September _____

April _____   October _____

May _____   November _____

June _____   December _____

Challenges:

Major _____

1st Sub-challenge _____

2nd Sub-challenge _____

YOUR PERSONAL CHART

Birthdate _____

Birth Number _____

Birth Sign _____

Birth Element _____

This planetary aspect represents the moral excellence and good-ness that the soul has achieved in former lifetimes, virtues which will assist a person in this lifetime.

Birth Musical Note _____

Personal Year for 1991 _____

Personal Year for 1992 _____

Personal Year for 1993 _____

Personal Year for 1994 _____

Personal Year for 1995 _____

Personal Year for 1996 _____

Personal Year for 1997 _____

Personal Year for 1998 _____

Personal Year for 1999 _____

Personal Year for 2000 _____

Personal Month Numbers:

January _____   July _____

February _____   August_____

March _____   September _____

April _____   October _____

May _____   November _____

June _____   December _____

Challenges:

Major _____

1st Sub-challenge _____

2nd Sub-challenge _____

YOUR PERSONAL CHART

Birthdate _____

Birth Number _____

Birth Sign _____

Birth Element _____

This planetary aspect represents the moral excellence and good-
ness that the soul has achieved in former lifetimes, virtues which
will assist a person in this lifetime.

Birth Musical Note _____

Personal Year for 1991 _____

Personal Year for 1992 _____

Personal Year for 1993 _____

Personal Year for 1994 _____

Personal Year for 1995 _____

Personal Year for 1996 _____

Personal Year for 1997 _____

Personal Year for 1998 _____

Personal Year for 1999 _____

Personal Year for 2000 _____

Personal Month Numbers:

January _____   July _____

February _____   August _____

March _____   September _____

April _____   October _____

May _____   November _____

June _____   December _____

Challenges:

Major _____

1st Sub-challenge _____

2nd Sub-challenge _____

YOUR PERSONAL CHART

Birthdate _____

Birth Number _____

Birth Sign _____

Birth Element _____

This planetary aspect represents the moral excellence and good-
ness that the soul has achieved in former lifetimes, virtues which
will assist a person in this lifetime.

Birth Musical Note _____

Personal Year for 1991 _____

Personal Year for 1992 _____

Personal Year for 1993 _____

Personal Year for 1994 _____

Personal Year for 1995 _____

Personal Year for 1996 _____

Personal Year for 1997 _____

Personal Year for 1998 _____

Personal Year for 1999 _____

Personal Year for 2000 _____

Personal Month Numbers:

January _____	July _____
February _____	August _____
March _____	September _____
April _____	October _____
May _____	November _____
June _____	December _____

Challenges:

Major _____

1st Sub-challenge _____

2nd Sub-challenge _____

YOUR PERSONAL CHART

Birthdate _____

Birth Number _____

Birth Sign _____

Birth Element _____

This planetary aspect represents the moral excellence and good-
ness that the soul has achieved in former lifetimes, virtues which
will assist a person in this lifetime.

Birth Musical Note _____

Personal Year for 1991 _____

Personal Year for 1992 _____

Personal Year for 1993 _____

Personal Year for 1994 _____

Personal Year for 1995 _____

Personal Year for 1996 _____

Personal Year for 1997 _____

Personal Year for 1998 _____

Personal Year for 1999 _____

Personal Year for 2000 _____

Personal Month Numbers:

January _____   July _____

February _____   August _____

March ____ _____   September _____

April _____   October _____

May _____   November _____

June _____   December _____

Challenges:

Major _____

1st Sub-challenge _____

2nd Sub-challenge _____

YOUR PERSONAL CHART

Birthdate _____

Birth Number _____

Birth Sign _____

Birth Element _____

This planetary aspect represents the moral excellence and goodness that the soul has achieved in former lifetimes, virtues which will assist a person in this lifetime.

Birth Musical Note _____

Personal Year for 1991 _____

Personal Year for 1992 _____

Personal Year for 1993 _____

Personal Year for 1994 _____

Personal Year for 1995 _____

Personal Year for 1996 _____

Personal Year for 1997 _____

Personal Year for 1998 _____

Personal Year for 1999 _____

Personal Year for 2000 _____

Personal Month Numbers:

January _____   July _____

February _____   August _____

March _____   September _____

April _____   October _____

May _____   November _____

June _____   December _____

Challenges:

Major _____

1st Sub-challenge _____

2nd Sub-challenge _____

YOUR PERSONAL CHART

Birthdate _____

Birth Number _____

Birth Sign _____

Birth Element _____

This planetary aspect represents the moral excellence and good-ness that the soul has achieved in former lifetimes, virtues which will assist a person in this lifetime.

Birth Musical Note _____

Personal Year for 1991 _____

Personal Year for 1992 _____

Personal Year for 1993 _____

Personal Year for 1994 _____

Personal Year for 1995 _____

Personal Year for 1996 _____

Personal Year for 1997 _____

Personal Year for 1998 _____

Personal Year for 1999 _____

Personal Year for 2000 _____

Personal Month Numbers:

January _____	July _____
February _____	August_____
March _____	September _____
April _____	October _____
May _____	November _____
June _____	December _____

Challenges:

Major _____

1st Sub-challenge _____

2nd Sub-challenge _____

YOUR PERSONAL CHART

Birthdate _____

Birth Number _____

Birth Sign _____

Birth Element _____

This planetary aspect represents the moral excellence and good-
ness that the soul has achieved in former lifetimes, virtues which
will assist a person in this lifetime.

Birth Musical Note _____

Personal Year for 1991 _____

Personal Year for 1992 _____

Personal Year for 1993 _____

Personal Year for 1994 _____

Personal Year for 1995 _____

Personal Year for 1996 _____

Personal Year for 1997 _____

Personal Year for 1998 _____

Personal Year for 1999 _____

Personal Year for 2000 _____

Personal Month Numbers:

January _____   July _____

February _____   August _____

March _____   September _____

April _____   October _____

May _____   November _____

June _____   December _____

Challenges:

Major _____

1st Sub-challenge _____

2nd Sub-challenge _____

YOUR PERSONAL CHART

Birthdate _____

Birth Number _____

Birth Sign _____

Birth Element _____

This planetary aspect represents the moral excellence and good-
ness that the soul has achieved in former lifetimes, virtues which
will assist a person in this lifetime.

Birth Musical Note _____

Personal Year for 1991 _____

Personal Year for 1992 _____

Personal Year for 1993 _____

Personal Year for 1994 _____

Personal Year for 1995 _____

Personal Year for 1996 _____

Personal Year for 1997 _____

Personal Year for 1998 _____

Personal Year for 1999 _____

Personal Year for 2000 _____

Personal Month Numbers:

January _____   July _____

February _____   August _____

March _____   September _____

April _____   October _____

May _____   November _____

June _____   December _____

Challenges:

Major _____

1st Sub-challenge _____

2nd Sub-challenge _____

THE PRACTICAL PSYCHIC
John Friedlander & Cynthia Pearson

● Practical techniques for enlisting the ●
resources of your own psychic ability

"How fascinating this book is—such a practical approach to the study of our nature that one wonders why no one has thought of doing it in just this way before!"

—Robert F. Butts, co-creator of the Seth books

"This book is spirited, spiritual and down-to-earth. The authors have done their homework—and a good deal more."

—Marilyn Ferguson, author of *The Aquarian Conspiracy*

"A wonderfully clear and inspiring book, full of valuable exercises and insights. The authors succeed in de-mystifying psychic work, making it accessible and empowering to the ordinary reader."

—Roger Woolger, Ph.D., author of *Other Lives, Other Selves*

John Friedlander, a graduate of Harvard Law School, channel, teacher and member of the original Jane Roberts/Seth classes teams up with Cynthia Pearson to teach psychic development. Step-by-step instructions are provided to help you unleash your psychic ability. You don't need to possess any special talents or abilities to be clairvoyant, telepathic, or precognitive. Read this book and bring your intuitive powers to life!

160 pp. ● ISBN 0-87728-728-7 ● Trade Paper, $9.95

"What's in a name?"
POTENTIAL
The Name Analysis Book
Paul and Valeta Rice

- Want to change your name?
- Or do you want to learn to live more comfortably with the one you've got?
- An easy-to-read guidebook that explains the universal meaning of your name.

Paul and Valeta Rice explore the depths of numerology to show you how your birth name holds the key to your inner self. They explain the numbers, master numbers and the special nuances of number combinations, so you can learn to analyze your name on many levels. Without having to know any complicated mathematical procedure, you will learn how to analyze:

- your desired self and dormant self
- your special abilities number
- your karmic number—and what you need to work on in this lifetime!
- the spiritual dimensions your name holds
- the layers of meaning you can derive from your name

With this book you will be able to discover what's in a name—and if you don't like the one you have, you can change it!

192 pp. • ISBN 0-87728-632-9 • Trade Paper, $8.95

WEISER ORDER FORM

Samuel Weiser, Inc.
Box 612, York Beach, Me 03910

You may use this form to order any of the Weiser publications listed in this book:

Title	Author	ISBN	Price

Shipping and handling: We ship UPS when possible so that lost shipments can be traced. Include $2.00 for orders under $10.00 and $3.00 for orders over $10.00.

Credit Card Orders: We accept MasterCard and Visa. Call to place your chargecard order: 1-800-423-7087.

☐ Please send me your free catalog.